IOWA'S FAIR

IOWA'S FAIR

PHOTOGRAPHS BY BILL WOOLSTON

Thorn Creek Press · Genesee Idaho

To my wife, Catherine

Printed in the United States of America
Library of Congress Catalogue Card Number 75-9404
I S B N 0-915664-01-1

FOREWORD

This book is about the people of *Iowa's Fair.* During the summer of 1972 I photographed at four fairs across the state of Iowa. My routine at each fair allowed me to photograph a large and varied group of people from early morning until late at night. Each of the images made was with the knowledge and consent of the individuals photographed.

This journey was, in part, an attempt to document the people of the traditional county fair before this viable institution vanished or radically changed. It was my hope that these images, at sometime, could be refered to as social documents of a passing phenomenon.

This journey was also, in part, a pursuit of an old memory of holding my father's hand and watching with open-mouthed amazement at the sights, sounds, and smells of the midway, the animals, and the crowds.

Bill Woolston
Oct 6 1975

Bill Woolston
Spring, 1975

Corn Seed Salesman, Clay County Fair

Randy and Nick, Lee County Fair

Father and Son, Lee County Fair

4-H Contestant, Lee County Fair

Helping Hand, Clay County Fair

Final Judging, Iowa State Fair

4-H Dairy Contestant, Iowa State Fair

Grandstand Crowd, Sheep Judging, Lee County Fair

Dairy Princess, Iowa State Fair

Hog Judging, Southern Iowa Fair

Hereford Queen, Iowa State Fair

Combine, Clay County Fair

Summer Trophies, Lee County Fair

Working in the Rain, Lee County Fair

Family Portrait, Southern Iowa Fair

Farm Family, Southern Iowa Fair

Pro Tattooist, Southern Iowa Fair

Pony Ride, Lee County Fair

Buttered Popcorn Booth, Iowa State Fair

Before the Talent Show, Iowa State Fair

Senior Portrait Specials, Southern Iowa Fair

Talent Show Audience, Iowa State Fair

Cookout King, Iowa State Fair

70 Blue Ribbons, Culinary Division, Iowa State Fair

Prize Winners, Iowa State Fair

Air Cavalry Recruiter, Iowa State Fair

Join the Marines, Southern Iowa Fair

Day Care on the Midway, Iowa State Fair

Cotton Candy, Iowa State Fair

Evening of a Long Day, Iowa State Fair

Melody, Iowa State Fair

Midway Children, Iowa State Fair

Dave, Gorham's Midway, Lee County Fair

Above the Midway, Lee County Fair

Speedball Operator, Iowa State Fair

Balloon Lady, Iowa State Fair

Zipper, Century 21 Midways, Iowa State Fair

Jim's Skyfighter Ride, Iowa State Fair

An Element of Risk, Iowa State Fair

Penny Arcade, Southern Iowa Fair

Gorilla Girl, Iowa State Fair

Three Graces, Iowa State Fair

House of Horrors, Iowa State Fair

Political Sticker, Iowa State Fair

Cutting up at the Midway, Iowa State Fair

Merry-go-Round, Lee County Fair

Neon Blues, Iowa State Fair

Trabant, Southern Iowa Fair

End of the day, Southern Iowa Fair

All photographs in this book were made with 35mm format handheld cameras, Nikon F and Nikkormat cameras were used with 35mm, 50mm, 105mm, and 200mm lenses. A Leica camera with 21mm, and 28mm lenses was also used.

All photographs were made with natural and/or available light.

The film used was Tri-X rated between 200 ASA and 400 ASA. The film was developed in D-76 for around 7 minutes.

This book is printed in Duo-tone by Rohner Printing Company, Chicago. Typeset by the News-Review Publishing Company, Moscow, Idaho.

Invaluable assistance in design and image selection: Harold Allen and Catherine Woolston.